The Pasolini Book

The Pasolini Book

Stacy Szymaszek

The Pasolini Book

Covers printed on French Paper by SpeeDeeQue, Durham, NC
Printed and bound by Maple Press, York, PA
First edition, 2022

ISBN-13: 978-0-9994313-8-2

The text is set in Janson, a typeface originally designed by Miklós Tótfalusi Kis after the Dutch Baroque style.

The cover is set in GT Sectra and Perpetua.

Photo Credits:
Page ix: Pier Paolo Pasolini, director, September 24, 1966
Photograph by Richard Avedon

Page x: Stacy Szymaszek, 2017
Photograph by Venn Daniel

The Golias Books device is taken from an illustration by François Desprez, spuriously attributed to Rabelais, in *Les Songes drolatiques de Pantagruel* (1565).

Designed and published by Golias Books
www.goliasbooks.com
N. Y. | N. C.

Contents

Note on the Text

This book is a collection of most of my writing from 2004–2020 that engages with the figure of Italian artist Pier Paolo Pasolini. I first encountered Pasolini's poems while working at Woodland Pattern Book Center in Milwaukee, WI. I remember the moment my coworker and friend Drew Kunz handed me *Roman Poems* (translated by Lawrence Ferlinghetti and Francesca Valente; preface by Alberto Moravia; City Lights, 1986) and said he thought I would like it. I was immediately taken by Pasolini's idea of civic poetry as well as a bit put off by what I then felt was overdone (i.e., sentimental) in the writing. I got into the nitty gritty of my particular response by taking each poem in *Roman Poems* and writing my own corresponding version, or what I thought of as emotional translations and, in retrospect, my earliest effort at exploring queer persona in serial work. Dana Ward published the collection, *Pasolini Poems*, with his imprint Cy Press in 2005. We decided to push my concept further by having the chapbook mimic the structure of *Roman Poems* as much as possible, with a black and white photo as cover and a preface. The repetition of this conceptual framework occasioned another preface for the 2020 version.

In 2010, I started writing "A Sentimental Education" (one of Pasolini's poem titles via Flaubert) which merged aspects of my autobiography, and some fabrication, with what I know about Pasolini's life and death. His murder, when I was 7 years old, in the piece, becomes an origin story for my fear of being punished "by man or God" for my queerness. I first wrote the piece as notes for a talk series called Tendencies. Then, I changed it and performed it at Poetry Time at Space Space. I changed it again and performed it for a series called 443 PAS. It was never the same piece twice and I never finished it. It became ephemeral. I am now declaring it *finito*. These 3 iterations of talks are presented here in a form that is an homage to another writer important to me, David Antin, though they were not improvised. Passages that repeat from piece to piece are retained but the text is grayed out.

In 2020, living in Tucson after receiving a grant for poetry from The Foundation for Contemporary Arts (FCA), I had the thought that I should do something with "A Sentimental Education," which had for years loomed as a novella I couldn't write properly until I had more time. But, as I found, that ship had sailed. As automatically as I'd started *Pasolini Poems* in 2004, I started *Pasolini Poems :: Divine Mimesis* (*The Divine Mimesis* is the title of another Pasolini book). Repeating the same method I'd used 16 years earlier, I wrote a new version of each poem in the City Lights book *Roman Poems*. I started writing in January, not before the Coronavirus pandemic, but just before it was known to the US public. I was drawn again to Pasolini to find an empathetic companion in my own blooming anti-institutional, anti-authoritarian stance, and to find out how much I had learned in my own trajectory as a self-declared civic poet. I wrote it as institutional structures in the field of literary arts, both loved and hated, and loved to hate, started to collapse in a way that could no longer be shielded from the public.

From 2011 to 2020, I applied, without success, for many residencies and grants so I could get myself to Rome to finish my Pasolini book. The FCA, an award I did not apply for, honored my body of work with a generous amount of money, but the pandemic was soon upon us and I knew that I would have to finish the book in the desert. It wasn't too challenging to make the circumstances work (deserts do feature in many of Pasolini's films) and it probably added a desired sensation of an awkward fit. I am not, after all, Pasolini, and none of these poems were written in Italy.

I'm grateful that the editors at Golias Books have honored what will likely be a project that goes on as long as I live, this waystation text, as a complete book *the way it came to be*—from the life of, what I can only believe most institutions are threatened by, a working poet.

SS
December 2021
New York

Pasolini Poems

(2005)

Preface to 2005 Cy Press Edition of *Pasolini Poems*

"One poet is not more valuable than another, but Pasolini has said more important things with greater force than others."
—Alberto Moravia

In introducing Stacy Szymaszek's *Pasolini Poems* I thought I should quote the man who introduced Pasolini's *Roman Poems*. Without doubt, Szymaszek set out to write her homage to Pasolini because of the importance and force of his words. Yet the resulting collection of poems is more complicated than the term *homage* suggests. The layers through which she writes include a knowledge of Pasolini as a filmmaker, a rivalry with masculinity, a loving portrait of Pasolini the man, and reflections on what it means to be a civic poet.

Szymaszek adheres to Pasolini's commitment to writing in the first person, a stringent, unapologetic song of herself. These "songs" represent a trustworthy conflation of emotional and social registers which is the duty of a civic poet. Yet, the chaos of Szymaszek's city, Milwaukee, is fictional compared to the chaos of Rome. In any city, there must be some chaos, it's just that ours is less colorful. As a result, Szymaszek's descriptions are often sardonic: "The city is celebrating another day of plumbing." More importantly though, the city of Szymaszek's poems may be less externalized than Pasolini's Rome. For one thing, she is female, and cannot wander with the freedom enjoyed by Pasolini. I would contend that Szymaszek's poems often reflect the city of desire rather than a love of a real place.

"Something I was devoted to just blustered away."

It is when Szymaszek chooses to quote Pasolini most directly, as in "Toward the Caracalla Baths," that I believe she is admitting to the gap between her contemporary female experience and his. That she as a midwestern American lesbian does not know what the era of bathhouses was really like, and that she thanks him for providing her a window into that other world. And yet, still later in "I Too Am…" Szymaszek rejoins Pasolini in their shared desire for coming out.

An option strangely more available to Szymaszek than to Pasolini, is to *BE* one of the boys Pasolini so admired, or even to *BE* his brother. Ironically, she is not so Other to these men as Pasolini seems to experience himself as being, those rough boys we see him regarding so lovingly in the black-and-white photographs in *Roman Poems*. It is the strength of the butch self-image, and the difference in our times, that allows Szymaszek that imaginative entry into commonplace masculinity.

Another layering of identification accomplished in *Pasolini Poems* is Szymaszek's loving scrutiny of Pasolini himself. In "To the Red Flag," note the shift in wording: Pasolini writes, "he who was covered with scabs is covered with wounds." Szymaszek writes, "he who is riddled with scabs is established in a wound." With this deft gesture I believe she is describing Pasolini and his prolific acts of creation. Both are also describing a flag, and we can agree that not much has changed since then. We are all still looking for a way to redeem the worth of our national and political banners.

Szymaszek's poems are annealed to Pasolini's through a shared rage. However, Szymaszek's rage is shorter and more to the point: she and her garden are one. I'll admit I identify with her rage more. But in Szymaszek's more shorthand methods one senses the necessarily competitive edge of this book-length *homage*. In "Rage," Szymaszek lays down the gauntlet: "I will grow sideburns." Pasolini was a man, after all, and so can she be, if she wants to. Szymaszek arrives at her personal apotheosis shortly afterward, with "Prayer to My Mother." The nature of her relationship to her mother is more liberatory and more openly angry. Szymaszek seems more free to step away from the ties that bind than Pasolini was. These are two very different mothers, whose levels of sacrifice and oppression speak to the gap between postwar Italy and millennial Milwaukee.

In Szymaszek's poems, her best lines are her own. She has buried them in the language of a poet she loves, but as she herself writes, "nothing can deceive those who are learned fugitives." Szymaszek lays bare the process by which a voice becomes its own, when the poet is willing to take as a point of departure the voice of another. We who remember Pasolini as much for his films as for his writing know that he too participated in that sort of homage with films like *The Thousand and One Nights*, *Decameron*, and *Medea*.

In the end, Szymaszek asks us to take another look at the tragic aspect of Pasolini the man. She writes of a "counter history of error / etched into the landscape / this countenance of a patient man." Pasolini dreamed of "the beautiful boys running in the light" of his last day on earth. Indeed, the beautiful boys ran, only not the way Pasolini so longed for: one ran away a murderer. But, as Stacy Szymaszek's last lines tell us, "desire without tragedy / is the practical end of poetry."

—Jennifer Montgomery

Diary

in the anxiety of
my transgression
I have never been touched
by remorse
here with you
in half-light
I feel no remorse
for the way
we use the government's
tongue but I do
feel anxious
as one who
will never grow up
feels anxious
about who will
care about them
here with you
making this movie
I don't think
we care about
each other
because we
are outlaws
and there
is no way for us
to care for long
don't you think?

The Holiday Over

behind a glass blower's window
a set of globlets I would have given
for an anniversary or a winter feast
I study their emulsion of light and air
to add to my account of this day

in the kitchen I listen
to another broadcast pledge
the more flimsy their lies become
the more people want to believe

_______________ will remain unaffected

the city's chaos thickens
spouses in neighboring apartments argue
the day is already ancient

from The Weeping of the Excavator

I return from the river
through a boarded-up arcade
I have a sack buried there
and inside a disguise

the city is celebrating
another day of plumbing
banners fly for a product
I've tried

moods wave against my face
an anthem in the wind
something I was devoted to
just blustered away

bartenders, hustlers, messengers!

our bodies will meet their murderers
but not tonight

Memories of Misery

Because something else still governs my heart
a stone building starts on fire in the forest
and I do not want to talk about it

Because something else still governs my heart
it is unsafe I cannot have my heart
acres of poor houses burn

Because acres of poor houses burn
and I watch them I survive on anxiety
how much life taken from me

Because a stone building starts on fire in the forest
the bread burns and the morning burns
all the wheat fields and deer burn

Because I cannot have my heart
I am paralyzed I cannot be trusted

The Wealth of Knowing

the Athenian is born in Athens a citizen

and when she travels she appears strange

every stranger is an autochthon of another land

that land is an absence which means all land

the veil of sky is perforated by shocks of memory

one regiment combats the illusion of the world with silence

Privilege of Thinking

to withdraw and think
to tell myself
to sit on a seat

I can think
forget hunger
forget senses
I'm wired
but still alive

working for a salary
it is implicit
I best not think

delicious
brown
rump

along pinstripes
in a friendly corner

my house is small
as a kennel
but I think
in infinite lessons

two eyes
a brain
and a name

hominiform
maneuvered by
a terrible pain

during the commute
a fragment
of aphorism

I surrender to
the thought
and hours

my coat loaded
with the money
of the world

Roman Evening

where are you going
when you go home?

I walk through
the hovels of Rome

buses full of people
going home

to their thousands of
kitchens
spouses
and sup

I'm wearing suede
and dark glasses

a target

with my defenses up

Toward the Caracalla Baths

they hold
in the folds
of their trousers
revelations they
want to share
in sweaters
the colors
of our country
they cleave
night air
warm with
red sage

he is reduced
to a scrap
iron chassis
of a body
in which
his old age
spills forth
his youth
a basin
of Vesuvian
oranges

his bare
chest smells
of animals
and holy ashes
here he is
smiling
under his
rough beret
Berber
shepherd

the
face
laughs
he
never
dies
who
was
never
born

Sex Consolation for Misery

I pencil in a Brindisi moustache
and go where one thinks the city ends
sending watchwords to the glinted

in the grace of love
the wretch feels himself a man

then is feared and despised
this is the nth onset of the city

secure in intrinsic blocs lovers confirm
there is hope in having no hope
—century, be silent
I have disguised myself
within your holographic light

and as a sculpture in acid rain
dissolve into the hush of discrepancy

Triumph of the Night

a pile of ruins
gather in truancy

empty porcelain
lit orange

collects
mercury

triumvirate optic
a forged Caravaggio

I was in the myriad
and no one knew

bitten by a lizard
sordid and governed

behind the petal
quiet and carbon

The Desire for Wealth of the Roman Lumpenproletariat

fruit of another history
the cigar lit in company is put out alone

beneath a carapace I think of how we are almost brothers
inscribed in the records of the same city structure

mafioso *bandit* *homo* *whore*

the windows are filthy
residential faces choose their phrases with immunity

the papistry is knocking on doors
delivering verbal directives

stay off the terrace
there will be no more buses to the sea
your daughter was observed

[ALL DIRECTIVES ARE NOW VERBAL]

I Too Am

I too am on the way to the baths
to free myself from the anxiety
of ancient illusions
my desires are humble
to wear a pressed cotton shirt
with comfortable shoes
to have a house in a district
where people say hello
a sun-warmed reading room
a balcony for roses
to think that a god
may still be in me...

I too have dreams that anchor me to the world
in my custom-made cabinet
how many drawers will I need?
one drawer for each manuscript
how many armchairs will I need?
one armchair for each friend
and in the bedroom a simple bed
covered by a flowery heirloom
then to sleep surrounded
by the paintings I love...

I too am on the way to the baths
to make my longing public

A Sentimental Education

Who was I at the time this film was made?

Our faces look mild but our passions are prehuman, dialogue
does not touch them.

By what standard am I guilty of not transforming my
affections into love?

Let's say, very guilty.

I feel gratitude toward the changing shape of the river bank,
too slow to feel or see.

I take comfort in the formal qualities of life.

Action was my constant dream.

I also wished to free myself from myself, that is to die. To die
in my creation…

I had just been delivered into a world that wasn't ideal and
realized the sorrowful gift of myself.

I was writing for someone who could only love me a great
deal.

In my language, a man was flowering.

There is the will to survive, which through grace becomes style.

The Resistance and Its Light

I came to the days of my resistance
with only a photograph in my wallet
of a Mediterranean mother and her child
in the style of Caravaggio, a style of fruit and light

accustomed to Italian fields, I carried a pistol
in a book, a feigned toughness became real
as I walked the streets with other boys
some of whom loved me

which often led to cruelty, the adrenaline
of escape, and other boys. Then men
who recited edicts wearing velvet, whose lips
never touched mine. Love was used for stature
a mythic play than ran every night

Tears

above is the black lid of recreated time
by brutal force I cauterize
the writing of memoir
tick of halogen erodes
images of aged tragedy
our death our survival
in the acrid morning
another civic phantom
tends to a piece of land

I am absorbed in an austere desire
to corrode narrative
muslin around my body
a bleached-out Rome
in the stupor of knowing
lapse in judgment is forever
all obsessions for which I lived
now a source of confined tears

To the Red Flag

You must exist so he can exist.

He who is riddled with scabs is established in a wound.

The writer becomes a vandal.

The vandal becomes a hero becomes a pusher becomes
a cat in the engine.

He sees valor in your colors and performs an anthem.

He falls in love and uses the language of buyers.

You are the empty Trojan horse he pushes.

Fragment: To Death

my feelings expire in light
fuel strata of burning leaves

doorman to my dog
who recognizes me not in name

we retread the path of runaways
occluded by filmic trees

I will not return to
your deformed calendar

of my fourteen thousand days
deafened by wind the hound guides

along any other course
my clothes could be

Rage

there was an exit from
the garden a sunken
passage for when you
knew its pale yellow
tranquility was
a façade

I tore a weave
of flowers from
a trellis my style
was never allowed
to form and wrapped
it about my neck
I will grow
sideburns

I Work All Day

I work all day in literature
and night styles me heroic
with mortared rose upon my breath
in an ancient fur-lined overcoat
nothing can mystify me
I hear windows being shot out
and don't bother with officials
I feel disgust yet continually
am charmed by letters and gifts
I watch myself being massacred
passive as a bird that carries
my heart to his home
leaving the rest of me to bureaucratic
dockets for identification

A Prayer to My Mother

if I were a son I might have the words
to say how my heart so little resembles

any other love and that you knew
and made it impenetrable

so I must tell you what is hard to know
from within your shelter my solemnity grew

the life you gave me is lonely as you
were lonely before I was born

but my distance is interminable
and without the distraction of births

or marriages, and I don't want to be alone
if I were a son I might have a penchant for travel

but my attachment is to the body
and the soul you bellowed into me

masters me in the privacy of this room
if I were one who prayed I would pray

don't die: future Julys lie in ruin

The Search for a Home

my thoughts are inmate to the city
its poorhouse sediment

there is luminous surface
over so much fatal error

another day of forbidden life
and no one is responsible

unable to bear plentitude
my homeopathy plentitude

which casts a dark sun
and radiates our fiction

But It Was a Naked and Swarming Italy

in a room with crumbling plaster my thoughts turned to my
appearance

my appearance as a man who was clean-shaven in a suit

the sound of kids playing was indistinguishable from a violent
dispute

dusk became operatic with mothers' voices

as television reporters alerted the public

walking in the city could be hazardous

a city that didn't depend on what I wrote about it

or how I wrote myself into it

or who I was when I left my room that night

Civil Song

luster of their mouths
perhaps after a first kiss
they return to their friends

in city coats and frayed trousers
already as discredited as old women
nothing can deceive fugitives

they return each other's kisses
who else would but them
one walks with a limp
the other finds it exciting

this no doubt the world will ignore

The Presence

what was gained is memory
the grueling soul feels saintly
a body lapsed in meaning
a mirror gave it ceremony
but well aware of its end

what matters is a story
that called for you
the aperture of tragedy
gradually absorbs salt
wakens in ruptured brightness

I manage to mother myself
yet cling to anything arousing
the desire to open my mouth
the wind makes me sicker
because I called it divine

Friulian Paintings

an overlay of perfumes
burns in the setting sun

I walk a familiar route
down the block where
porches have wind chimes
across asphalt lots
teenagers pass lost in thought
what a good idea
to undo every defense
with my own smile

dock workers lean
against handlebars

do you remember
our evening in Ruda?
the street fair made our
dreams seems possible

harvesters meet
at the edge
of a concealed place

men make love in alleys
having learned
to breathe quietly

nightfall is the siren
that activates these motions

I might be one of them
tomorrow or the next day
but I continue my walk
try to appear natural

Song of Bells

afternoon blackens
the city edged
by sulfuric plates
through the heat
of ideas I bring you
humanly nearer
bells in their measure
counterhistory of error
etched into landscape
the countenance
of a patient man

Day of My Death

in a city, not Trieste
                    nor Ostia
along a plowed boulevard
when night is prolonged
and salt fills my shoes
my body will burn
                    under a ready moon
                    hypothermic and full
my eyes will become weapons
the civilian sky will barrel with splendor

along a boulevard tarred and smooth
                              I'll fall burning
                              a mortal incense
avert your senses
except for you, beautiful boys
with camera minds
and curls on your brows
you will gather in that light

Reality

my body surges with anxiety
smothers itself with affinity
oh practical end of poetry

I search my ancestry for those
who worked without dignity
oh practical end of poetry

the sea-lit sky in elegiac span
where I see poet friends I've lost
their salt healed faces

poets who will never be parents
my words reveal the fantasy
then the practical end of poetry

at thirty-three I deliver my cognizance
to the obscure child made ill by light
I'm kneeling in confession till the end of my life

in the cut grass of an old July night
my destiny is not mediocrity
oh practical end of poetry

all around me the chorus of the happy
for whom reality is a friend

sun-washed and built the world is within

their landslide of flowers
and desire without tragedy
is the practical end of poetry

A Sentimental Education

(2010–2011)

May 6, 2010 Tendencies talk series with CA Conrad & Jack Kimball
CUNY Graduate Center, Manhattan

it was just after all soul's day, november 2nd, 1975. i was 6. the man i would become was murdered outside of rome, images of his crushed body broadcast worldwide, and no one in my house noticed or could have cared. my family lived in a suburb separated from others by wide belts of undeveloped land. it was organized by section and each section was designated a letter that every street name began with; we lived in the g-section on glen flora drive. the alphabetical logic was meant to give the families living there a sense of natural order and local cohesion. it felt like a gated community, but there was no need for a gate. trespassers were always immediately detected and observed. the gate existed in my subconscious and though i never got close enough, i knew an electric current ran through it. in 1982, my mother chaperoned our class boat ride on lake michigan, and, seeing me among my peers, registered to what extent my clothes distinguished me from them. i went to a catholic grade school where we all had to wear navy slacks and yellow, white or green polo shirts, so the problem was really one of style; my black suede shoes and the tattered holes in my shirts where i removed the designer's insignias with scissors. she drew me aside at the prow of the boat to ask me, "why won't you wear chinos and loafers like the other girls?" i took my eyes off of her, furiously, and focused past the breakwater, clenched my teeth and said, "i'm not like other girls." i want very much to remember what happened next. did i have a hard time sleeping that night? i didn't know the implications of the 5 words i pronounced to my mother—a message veiled to myself but plain to her. as i found out much later, she cried herself to sleep that night, her fear of what i was had been confirmed. i noted that she intensified her surveillance of me, and her guardianship, as i was both a threat and in need of protection.

i became aware of my own mortality when the man i would become, pier paolo pasolini, was found murdered on the beach in the port town of ostia.

human children are protected from the harsh realities of life by the prolongation of parental care but what happens when there is an attempt at over-protection, when an already unearthly atmosphere becomes ever more divorced from reality? instead of an erotic blossoming, i underwent an erotic implosion, my magical mythical childhood was imbued with the opposite of anarchy—an impossible future. in first grade, my friend and i stared at each other's vaginas beneath her basement steps. then, i went home and took a scissor to all of the halter-tops in my drawer and was punished.

i didn't think my desire could ever lead to other bodies until i found out about the man i would become, pier paolo pasolini, whose body was found battered on wasteland near the sea.

i had a recurring dream throughout the 80s where i came upon an unknown woman face-down in a parking lot. i wondered if she was injured and went to her and turned her over whereupon we started kissing. at that point i always woke up, as one wakes from a nightmare right before something bad happens. my 7th grade religion teacher handed out blank books to my class so we could write about our relationships with god. it was then that i decided to keep a record of my thinking. writing about my feelings for god would have made one of my dilemmas discoverable. too dangerous. i often had a hard time falling asleep after my catholic education had commenced. i laid in bed engaged in roulette with love and hate: *i love god, i hate god, i love god, i hate god…* . whichever declaration resounded in my head right before i fell asleep was the truth. when i went to my first confession at 8 years old, i didn't understand that i was a sinner, that my game put my soul in further jeopardy. i waited in line for the booth's green light to flash, entered, and sat in silence for a moment before i made up some mild but poor behavior so the priest could restore my inner grace.

my report cards often contained "additional comments" from my teachers about needing to smile more, which confused me since knowledge of death and suffering were part of my studies with the catholics. i memorized the 7 sayings jesus spoke on the cross as he died; i made them mine. one is, "i thirst." it must have been the last since, as the shortest, it would require the least amount of air to say. when he arose from the dead easter morning he said to mary magdalene, "don't touch me," and i issued this warning as well. either i was going to hurt someone or i was going to be hurt. with the warning came a look, a death look. i didn't want to be a girl but i never wanted to be a boy. i was a progressive mutation without a functional notion of my identity. i discovered i could contain the fear and hatred of my community. for a period of 2 years my house was vandalized by a group of enemy girls but i pretended i didn't know their names to keep my parents from reporting them. i didn't need them to be punished. i used my physical prowess in backyard games of football where i could hurl my body into the bodies of younger boys.

pier paolo pasolini used his art to express the virtues of people who are excluded or forgotten by the center. i was at the dinner table, the sun going down and the light from the hall casting some light on the page of homework. my father asked "how can you be so dumb?," cracked a pencil in my face and disappeared into his basement workshop, the sounds of sawing and sanding came up through the vents. i didn't have an answer. i never loved a class till i loved junior high history class but was crestfallen that our teacher preferred to call on boys as well as reward his favorites with gifts that he kept locked in a closet at the back of the classroom. he liked athletic boys but i too was athletic, winning 1st place ribbons in all of the school's olympic day events that year. this teacher, also apparently unimpressed by my paper on theodore roosevelt, complete with portrait of him that i sketched in pencil, told my parents that i was a follower and not a leader. he advised them to enroll me in a catholic high school so i wouldn't come under poor influence. one of my most beloved possessions was a portfolio of glossy portraits of all 36 presidents. i turned my closet into an office and worked on memorizing their biographies.

pasolini (1922–1975), italian, best known in the united states as a poet and filmmaker, was also a journalist, philosopher, linguist, novelist, actor, painter and political figure. his father came from ancient nobility, was in the italian army and was famous for having saved mussolini's life. his mother was a teacher from a peasant family that had risen to petite bourgeois status. ill-suited for each other, they married under social pressure. pasolini assimilated their tensions profoundly. he recalled that in order to medicate an infection in his eye his father held him down by force. from then on all his life revolved around his mother—susanna—and he thought of the family as an archaic remnant.

in 1984, i became a freshman at greendale high school and quickly realized one of the behaviors my mother feared. i broke curfew for the first time and drank with the kids who hung out in the woods by the river. i was wasted the first time i made out with someone, a boy who was later expelled. i came home with my new white canvas shoes coated in mud. my mother was vigilant in her nightgown at the front window between the curtain and the glass. my father didn't care about this type of disobedience. not saying please and thank you, or not putting something away properly could start a fight, but in his mind breaking curfew didn't have any bearing on the quality of your adult character. it's just what kids did. it's what he did. i went on this way for months, till the departure from what i understood to be my self felt on the one hand too extreme and on the other hand not the radical change i was searching for. i was heading into an identifiable category of kid, the burn-out. my need to self-regulate kicked in and an answer came in the form of membership in my school's group against drinking where everyone found me to be edgy and unpredictable. i made an entry in my book about renouncing one thing for another thing—the thinking given to me by the catholics who taught me for 8 years. i later found out that the first boy i dated, during this period of drinking in the woods, committed suicide after high school. he was the first of several troubled men i would become erotically involved with. most of the kids in my school's anti-drinking program drank, they just wore nice clothes and got good grades. i wasn't invested in either, but i had a vision of the person i wanted to be and that person understood that sometimes people have to make certain concessions in order to get closer to what they want. i had to go clothes shopping with my new friends. the flight pants and t-shirts i wore my freshman year were replaced with anything made by esprit and forenza. i looked more like "one of the girls" but this conformity served to conceal inner change, the man I was becoming.

my girlfriends loved me. and i loved them. i had never had a group of friends and my house quickly became the favorite for slumber parties. one night we watched the horror film *the little girl who lived down the lane*. my 4 new friends clung to me as we tried to anticipate how jodie foster became an orphan. my breasts were already big, to my dismay, but my friends dove into my embrace –made happy by my amplitude. i had no idea what "butch" was but this was one of my first emotional experiences of it. for valentine's day they wrote me notes about how special i was and sent me dyed carnations. i loved one girl especially, and when we held hands in bed i assured her it didn't mean i was a lesbian. she spoke german and wanted me to go to on a summer trip to berlin but i thought it was too dangerous for me to travel; the plane would crash, or i would be lost and wouldn't be able to speak or be understood. it was difficult for news to reach me in the 80s. i spent a lot of time in my bedroom listening to records that seemed to reach the midwest years after they had became popular elsewhere. i also graduated from a high school that didn't teach us about the holocaust, the israelis and the palestinians, or the cold war. i was particularly attuned to events that affirmed that the world was dangerous place, and vividly remembered news of the assassination of john lennon, and the attempts on ronald reagan and pope john paul ii. i noted that the people around me had contempt for reality. maybe i did too. in retrospect, there were opportunities for me to make a break, but i had created a way to cope. when the berlin wall came down in 1989, i saved the issue of *time magazine* with a group of reveling young people on it and thought of my friend.

in christina rossetti's "goblin market," the weakened sister, laura, eats the fruit that the goblin men pummeled lizzie with, and undergoes a transformation of such intensity that her life hangs in the balance, though the next morning she returns to her old self. it was my 1st year at my local university and i stopped writing in my book and started writing poems. i found a room in a huge east side apartment with a ballet dancer who was rarely there, a graduate student in film, and someone who worked for the symphony orchestra. they were all older than me and i tried to conceal how little i knew about how to function in the world. i wanted a type of transformation where i would not return to my old self in the morning. my parents gave me a used car, and were paying my tuition. i worked part-time with a group of artists, musicians, painters, writers, and other weirdos at oriental drugs, on a corner that formed the epicenter of alternative culture. one of the women i worked with asked me if i wanted to hang out. we went for a walk by the lake one night after our shift. she said between drags of her cigarette, "it's hard, isn't it?" i furrowed my brow. —"hard?" —"being gay." —"oh, yah, it is," pretending that of course i was gay and everyone knew it. i went back to her dorm and had sex with her. after a short period of dating, we got an apartment together. many of my poor decisions came from overly magical thinking; because she recognized me, i had to spend my life with her. but i was not equipped to handle her mental illness, substance abuse, and the care she demanded. she eventually slept with a friend of hers and i took it as a legitimate reason to move out. for the next 15 years, i renounced "relationships" in favor of the sexual exploit. i thought it meant that i was not repressed, that at least that i had a body willing to die, a body that didn't need to make history. some people feel that pasolini organized his own immolation. can an expressive strategy provoke death? ward off death? my body was a constant offering to the enemy and was being overprotected. i started sketching copies of one of pasolini's self-portraits, got some clear glasses to wear since i had 20/20 vision, and read books that were important to him, such as *life against death* and *the sacred and the profane*. a psychic risk allowed me to turn the fear of my fate into work. the fundamental rule of alchemy is secrecy, for which i have a perverse love. the word "manifesto" is derived from the latin "manifestum," meaning clear or plainly guilty. poetic masks offer me both modi operandi.

after i left home as a young adult, i came upon a quote by albert Einstein with a beginning very familiar to my ears: "the world is a dangerous place to live," but his statement concluded with: "not because of the people who are evil, but because of the people who don't do anything about it." the plot of pasolini's 1968 film *teorema* features a mysterious stranger, played by terence stamp, who appears in the lives of a bourgeois family, has sexual affairs with all of them, then disappears. god, devil, or hustler? i have never rendered any of my lovers catatonic, sanctified, or mad, but i related to stamp's character as someone who can never be more than a visitor. the film ends tragically with the family incapable of understanding and resolving their experience with something sacred. in 1991, after i had moved 708 miles away, i had an argument on the phone with my mother and that night dreamed that the mafia was after me. my mother's family is sicilian but not mafia. i had to call them and make it right. the argument was about the month of july, the month i was born, and where i would spend it.

in pasolini's poem, "prayer for my mother," i predict a future where this month is a land in ruination with me as its ambassador. pasolini's murder is a cold case, a political killing that preyed upon his homosexuality. i'm among the majority who don't believe the convicted 17-year-old male prostitute committed the murder, at least not alone. pasolini was a towering embodiment of someone who knew that no religious belief, academic discipline, or intellectual attitude was free from the blindness of conformity. and he was often ambiguous and contradictory. he began his poem, "a sentimental education," with the line "chi fui?" "who was i?" in the 15th century people started to believe that a person's life flashed before their eyes at the moment of death, and that moment would give her biography its final meaning. poetry and film, are able to undo the work of time, restore the blank page of existence, and reintegrate it into the present. any form that can do this can alter the human body. "who was i?" is always a question in need of asking. i want to be delivered into the world again, maybe not less sorrowful, but fully active, against the fascist moment.

this is how i plan to continually emerge from the grave of my childhood.

A SENTIMENTAL EDUCATION

Who was I at the time this film was made?

Our faces look mild but our passions are pre-human, dialogue doesn't touch them.

By what standard am I guilty of not transforming my affections into love?

Let's say, very guilty.

I feel gratitude toward the changing shape of the riverbank, too slow to feel or see.

I take comfort in the formal qualities of life.

Action was my constant dream.

I also wished to free myself from myself, that is, to die. To die in my creation…

I'd just been delivered into a world that wasn't ideal and realized the sorrowful gift of oneself.

I was writing for someone who could only love me a great deal.

In my language, a man was flowering.

There is the will to survive, which through grace becomes style.

March 26, 2011

Poetry Time at Space Space with Will Edmiston, CA Conrad, & Lindsey Bolt
A house in Ridgewood, Queens

it was just after all soul's day, november 2nd, 1975. i was 6. the man i would become was murdered outside of rome, images of his crushed body broadcast worldwide, and no one in my house noticed or could have cared. my family lived in a suburb separated from others by wide belts of undeveloped land. it was organized by section and each section was designated a letter that every street name began with; we lived in the g-section on glen flora drive. the alphabetical logic was meant to give the families living there a sense of natural order and local cohesion. it felt like a gated community, but there was no need for a gate. trespassers were always immediately detected and observed. the gate existed in my subconscious and though i never got close enough, i knew an electric current ran through it. in 1982, my mother chaperoned our class boat ride on lake michigan, and, seeing me among my peers, registered to what extent my clothes distinguished me from them. i went to a catholic grade school where we all had to wear navy slacks and yellow, white or green polo shirts, so the problem was really one of style; my black suede shoes and the tattered holes in my shirts where i removed the designer's insignias with scissors. she drew me aside at the prow of the boat to ask me, "why won't you wear chinos and loafers like the other girls?" i took my eyes off of her, furiously, and focused past the breakwater, clenched my teeth and said, "i'm not like other girls." i want very much to remember what happened next. did i have a hard time sleeping that night? i didn't know the implications of the 5 words i pronounced to my mother—a message veiled to myself but plain to her. as i found out much later, she cried herself to sleep that night, her fear of what i was had been confirmed. i noted that she intensified her surveillance of me, and her guardianship, as i was both a threat and in need of protection.

i became aware of my own mortality when the man i would become, pier paolo pasolini, was found murdered on the beach in the port town of ostia.

human children are protected from the harsh realities of life by the prolongation of parental care but what happens when there is an attempt at over-protection, when an already unearthly atmosphere becomes ever more divorced from reality? instead of an erotic blossoming, i underwent an erotic implosion, my magical mythical childhood was imbued with the opposite of anarchy—an impossible future. in first grade, my friend and i stared at each other's vaginas beneath her basement steps. then, i went home and took a scissor to all of the halter-tops in my drawer and was punished.

i didn't think my desire could ever lead to other bodies until i found out about the man i would become, pier paolo pasolini, whose body was found battered on wasteland near the sea.

i had a recurring dream throughout the 80s where i came upon an unknown woman face-down in a parking lot. i wondered if she was injured and went to her and turned her over whereupon we started kissing. at that point i always woke up, as one wakes from a nightmare right before something bad happens. my 7th grade religion teacher handed out blank books to my class so we could write about our relationships with god. it was then that i decided to keep a record of my thinking. writing about my feelings for god would have made one of my dilemmas discoverable. too dangerous. i often had a hard time falling asleep after my catholic education had commenced. i laid in bed engaged in roulette with love and hate: *i love god, i hate god, i love god, i hate god…* . whichever declaration resounded in my head right before i fell asleep was the truth. when i went to my first confession at 8 years old, i didn't understand that i was a sinner, that my game put my soul in further jeopardy. i waited in line for the booth's green light to flash, entered, and sat in silence for a moment before i made up some mild but poor behavior so the priest could restore my inner grace.

my report cards often contained "additional comments" from my teachers about needing to smile more, which confused me since knowledge of death and suffering were part of my studies with the catholics. i memorized the 7 sayings jesus spoke on the cross as he died; i made them mine. one is, "i thirst." it must have been the last since, as the shortest, it would require the least amount of air to say. when he arose from the dead easter morning he said to mary magdalene, "don't touch me," and i issued this warning as well. either i was going to hurt someone or i was going to be hurt. with the warning came a look, a death look. i didn't want to be a girl but i never wanted to be a boy. i was a progressive mutation without a functional notion of my identity. i discovered i could contain the fear and hatred of my community. for a period of 2 years my house was vandalized by a group of enemy girls but i pretended i didn't know their names to keep my parents from reporting them. i didn't need them to be punished. i used my physical prowess in backyard games of football where i could hurl my body into the bodies of younger boys.

pier paolo pasolini used his art to express the virtues of people who are excluded or forgotten by the center. i was at the dinner table, the sun going down and the light from the hall casting some light on the page of homework. my father asked "how can you be so dumb?," cracked a pencil in my face and disappeared into his basement workshop, the sounds of sawing and sanding came up through the vents. i didn't have an answer. i never loved a class till i loved junior high history class but was crestfallen that our teacher preferred to call on boys as well as reward his favorites with gifts that he kept locked in a closet at the back of the classroom. he liked athletic boys but i too was athletic, winning 1st place ribbons in all of the school's olympic day events that year. this teacher, also apparently unimpressed by my paper on theodore roosevelt, complete with portrait of him that i sketched in pencil, told my parents that i was a follower and not a leader. he advised them to enroll me in a catholic high school so i wouldn't come under poor influence. one of my most beloved possessions was a portfolio of glossy portraits of all 36 presidents. i turned my closet into an office and worked on memorizing their biographies.

pasolini (1922–1975), italian, best known in the united states as a poet and filmmaker, was also a journalist, philosopher, linguist, novelist, actor, painter and political figure. his father came from ancient nobility, was in the italian army and was famous for having saved mussolini's life. his mother was a teacher from a peasant family that had risen to petite bourgeois status. ill-suited for each other, they married under social pressure. pasolini assimilated their tensions profoundly. he recalled that in order to medicate an infection in his eye his father held him down by force. from then on all his life revolved around his mother—susanna—and he thought of the family as an archaic remnant. he spent summers in susanna's rural birthplace, the motherland, and wrote his first book of poetry, *poesie a casarsa*, in the friulian peasant language he picked up from her. perhaps his identification with the poor came from sharing in a feeling of oppression. in his early 20s he ran a makeshift school for the local children in casarsa. he had kept his homosexuality a secret until 1949, when accusations that he had approached a male student led to the loss of his teaching job and his membership in the italian communist party. this began a lifetime of his detractors using his homosexuality to obscure their true political motivations. pasolini moved with his mother to rome. some accounts used the word "moved" but he used the word "escaped." one biographical note says he became immersed in the city's slum life. an oblique way of saying that he followed the ancient and profound call of city to homosexual, where his desire outside the laws of desire could flourish yet at the same time be driven toward the underworld, where he would meet the beautiful young boys with curls on their brows. his type.

pasolini cast susanna, his mother, as the older mary in his 1964 film *the gospel according to st. matthew*. a dark veil accentuates the structure of her face, which is the structure of his face. i've read books that say this is pasolini likening himself to jesus, but when i saw it, i felt that it was about pasolini using film to visually connect himself to his ideal—women, his mother, *the* mother. i think this because in his unfinished posthumously published text, *petrolio*, carlo has to become a woman to attain authenticity. pasolini and his mother were a couple; they shared a household until his death. to break their symbiotic relationship would have rendered her life force inaccessible to him but to sustain it required sacrifice.

when i became pasolini, i could not abide by this conflict.

there were some things that i wanted to be discovered, and i knew that my blank book could function as a depository for messages to my mother. i wrote in all caps: *i have a theory about my mom and dad*, but then didn't write anything else. i lacked the vocabulary and the skill to synthesize what i saw, but i wanted her to know that i knew things about her too. i slowly became a better writer and was able to compose short letters in my book to dr. paulina kernberg, whose column, "good vibrations," i followed in *dynamite* magazine. i addressed these letters to her and put the envelopes in our mailbox, but i either didn't know or didn't care that letters needed stamps. they met their intended recipient when my mother removed them, read them, and destroyed them. at school, we had our recess on a blacktop lot. i usually just sat on the curb by myself and waited for the bell to ring. once, i saw my mother standing alone off in the distance, watching me, alone.

it won't be surprising to hear that i read a lot, but around this time, i sensed i needed a different kind of book. our local drugstore sold some popular pocket paperbacks. i went in for my regular fare of baseball cards and gum but with a few extra dollars for *psycho-cybernetics* by maxwell maltz, a cosmetic surgeon who developed a system of ideas through which, he claimed, people could remove their emotional scars. he found that even after a successful procedure, many of his patients had unsatisfied expectations. he taught them to visualize the people they wanted to be, and that a person's outer success could never rise above the one visualized internally. i didn't know what a poet was but i began to feel that my imagination could signal the way to a fate different from those in my childhood community. i had not yet encountered the people i wanted to be.

pasolini wrote a poem called "prayer to my mother" which i first read in *roman poems*, a selected for english readers published in 1986. i read the book and didn't think it was that good, but then i read it again and thought it was good, but i wanted to write it myself casting myself as pasolini. i called it *pasolini poems*. in pasolini's "prayer" he tells susanna that she is irreplaceable. "and for this / the life you gave me is condemned to solitude." while he says he has a hunger for love and doesn't want to be alone, he strangely accepts their bondage, begging her not to desire death. i think pasolini was considered controversial because he didn't pretend to be interested in resolving his inner conflicts—he developed schema for them.

one of my mother's habitual expressions was "the world is a dangerous place to live." i knew this to be true through living with my father, who had a volatile temper. it was a seamless transition in his mind to yell at me and, shortly thereafter approach me jovially, "want to play catch?" I delivered a daily message to him through my eyes. *my will power is as great as yours.* one of the things he couldn't tolerate was "a half-assed job." i had a lot of anxiety around performing my chores to his satisfaction. when i ran over his newly planted shrubs with the tractor mower and got sent to my room, instead of resolving to do better i resolved to do less and do it slower. i became so inefficient that my mother ended up covering for me.

we had an english springer spaniel for about 6 months, a breed of gun dog traditionally used for flushing and retrieving game. i had been hunting with my father many times and saw that he was a good shot with gun and bow. we got along well in the town of wild rose, where he killed whatever animal was in season, cooked it, and served it. springers are rambunctious and no one in my family properly trained him. my mother wasn't a dog person and was home with him the most. i once witnessed my dad kick him down the stairs. later that week, when the dog misbehaved, i hit his hind end with his leash and was overcome with horror. when my mother, crying, told me that a family from the country was coming to adopt him, i didn't cry. i walked him to an overgrown row of lilac bushes that marked our lot line and said goodbye to him in private.

my parents wanted me to attend a high school called pius, but they didn't insist. my experience at st. alphonsus ungrounded my mother's faith in the church just enough, and my father was the first person i heard called "heathen." i conflated this with another notion i had about him. sometimes when i was mad at him i would ask my mother if she knew she was married to a cro-magnon man. after a pause, in which she made the decision not to admonish me, we both burst into laughter. there were other incidents when she issued an inside joke in his presence to make him feel out of place. one of her culinary specialties was stuffed artichokes but she wouldn't make one for him saying, "no carciofo for the medigan," "medigan" is southern italian slang for a person who is not Italian, like she and his children were. he sat eating his dish of pasta and sauce, his boney brow covering his eyes so i could never detect the nuances of how he felt.

in 1984, i became a freshman at greendale high school and quickly realized one of the behaviors my mother feared. i broke curfew for the first time and drank with the kids who hung out in the woods by the river. i was wasted the first time i made out with someone, a boy who was later expelled. i came home with my new white canvas shoes coated in mud. my mother was vigilant in her nightgown at the front window between the curtain and the glass. my father didn't care about this type of disobedience. not saying please and thank you, or not putting something away properly could start a fight, but in his mind breaking curfew didn't have any bearing on the quality of your adult character. it's just what kids did. it's what he did. i went on this way for months, till the departure from what i understood to be my self felt on the one hand too extreme and on the other hand not the radical change i was searching for. i was heading into an identifiable category of kid, the burn-out. my need to self-regulate kicked in and an answer came in the form of membership in my school's group against drinking where everyone found me to be edgy and unpredictable. i made an entry in my book about renouncing one thing for another thing—the thinking given to me by the catholics who taught me for 8 years. i later found out that the first boy i dated, during this period of drinking in the woods, committed suicide after high school. he was the first of several troubled men i would become erotically involved with.

May 28, 2011

443 PAS series with Robert Glück
443 Park Avenue South, Manhattan

it was just after all soul's day, november 2nd, 1975. i was 6. the man i would become was murdered outside of rome, images of his crushed body broadcast worldwide, and no one in my house noticed or could have cared. my family lived in a suburb separated from others by wide belts of undeveloped land. it was organized by section and each section was designated a letter that every street name began with; we lived in the g-section on glen flora drive. the alphabetical logic was meant to give the families living there a sense of natural order and local cohesion. it felt like a gated community, but there was no need for a gate. trespassers were always immediately detected and observed. the gate existed in my subconscious and though i never got close enough, i knew an electric current ran through it. in 1982, my mother chaperoned our class boat ride on lake michigan, and, seeing me among my peers, registered to what extent my clothes distinguished me from them. i went to a catholic grade school where we all had to wear navy slacks and yellow, white or green polo shirts, so the problem was really one of style; my black suede shoes and the tattered holes in my shirts where i removed the designer's insignias with scissors. she drew me aside at the prow of the boat to ask me, "why won't you wear chinos and loafers like the other girls?" i took my eyes off of her, furiously, and focused past the breakwater, clenched my teeth and said, "i'm not like other girls." i want very much to remember what happened next. did i have a hard time sleeping that night? i didn't know the implications of the 5 words i pronounced to my mother—a message veiled to myself but plain to her. as i found out much later, she cried herself to sleep that night, her fear of what i was had been confirmed. i noted that she intensified her surveillance of me, and her guardianship, as i was both a threat and in need of protection.

i became aware of my own mortality when the man i would become, pier paolo pasolini, was found murdered on the beach in the port town of ostia.

human children are protected from the harsh realities of life by the prolongation of parental care but what happens when there is an attempt at over-protection, when an already unearthly atmosphere becomes ever more divorced from reality? instead of an erotic blossoming, i underwent an erotic implosion, my magical mythical childhood was imbued with the opposite of anarchy—an impossible future. in first grade, my friend and i stared at each other's vaginas beneath her basement steps. then, i went home and took a scissor to all of the halter-tops in my drawer and was punished.

i didn't think my desire could ever lead to other bodies until i found out about the man i would become, pier paolo pasolini, whose body was found battered on wasteland near the sea, was discovered near the town's docks, was found by the police near a wharf in ostia, on the outskirts of rome.

my 7th grade religion teacher handed out blank books to my class so we could write about our relationships with god. it was then that i decided to keep a record of my thinking. writing about my feelings for god would have made one of my dilemmas discoverable, too dangerous. i often had a hard time falling asleep after my catholic education had commenced. i laid in bed engaged in roulette with love and hate: *i love god, i hate god, i love god, i hate god*. . . . the declaration resounding in my head right before i fell asleep was the truth. when i went to my first confession at 8 years old, i didn't understand that i was a sinner, that my game put my soul in further jeopardy. i waited in line for the booth's green light to flash, entered, and sat in silence for a moment before i made up some mild but poor behavior so the priest could restore my inner grace. i didn't want to be a girl but i never wanted to be a boy. i was a progressive mutation without a functional notion of my identity. i discovered i could contain the fear and hatred of my community. for a period of 2 years my house was vandalized by a group of enemy girls but i pretended i didn't know their names to keep my parents from reporting them. i didn't need them to be punished. what i remember about being young is the sensation of having a broad presence that felt at odds with my need to recede. mostly a bedroom dweller, during the summer of 1980, at age 11, adeptness overcame my body and i set out into the neighborhood to find boys. i honed my physical prowess in backyard games of football. i was physically struck by their bodies, attracted by their legs, by the hollow of their knees. i accessed their bodies by hurling mine at their calves, bringing them down in the tackle. each time i became more like them, but then everyone changed.

on the morning of november 2nd 1975, on the roman litoral of ostia, in an uncultivated field in via dell'idroscalo, a woman, maria teresa lollobrigida, discovered the dead body of the man i would become.

there were some things that i wanted to be discovered, and i knew that my blank books could function as a depository for messages to my mother. i wrote in capital letters: i wrote in all caps: *i have a theory about my mom and dad*, but then didn't write anything else. i lacked the vocabulary and the skill to synthesize what i saw, but i wanted her to know that i knew things about her too. i slowly became a better writer and was able to compose short letters to dr. paulina kernberg, whose column, "good vibrations," i followed in *dynamite* magazine. i addressed these letters to her and put the envelopes in our mailbox, but i either didn't know or didn't care that letters needed stamps. they met their intended recipient when my mother removed them, read them, and destroyed them. at school, we had our recess on a blacktop lot. i usually just sat on the curb by myself and waited for the bell to ring. once, i saw my mother standing alone off in the distance, watching me, alone.

pasolini (1922–1975), italian, best known in the united states as a filmmaker, was also a poet, journalist, philosopher, linguist, novelist, actor, painter and political figure. his father came from ancient nobility, was in the italian army and famously saved mussolini's life. his mother was a teacher from a peasant family that had risen to petite bourgeois status. his father loved his mother more than she loved him. he was fascist and she was antifascist. pasolini assimilated their tensions profoundly. at the age of 3 pasolini underwent a crisis that he would analyze for the rest of his life. while his mother was pregnant with his brother, he started to suffer from eye infections. his father held him down by force on the kitchen table, opened his eye with his fingers, and put "collyrium" (eye wash) in. "it was from that symbolic moment that i began not to love my father." he spent summers in susanna's rural birthplace, and wrote his first book of poetry, *poesie a casarsa*, in the friulian peasant language he picked up from her. in his early 20s he ran a makeshift school for the local children in casarsa. he had kept his homosexuality a secret until 1949, when accusations that he had approached a male student led to the loss of his teaching job and his membership in the italian communist party. his detractors easily used his homosexuality to obscure their political motivations. pasolini moved with his mother to rome. some accounts used the word "moved" but he used the word "escaped." one biographical note says he became immersed in the city's slum life. an oblique way of saying that he followed the ancient and profound call of city to homosexual. rome. where he would meet the beautiful young boys with curls on their brows. his type.

pasolini cast susanna, as the older mary in his 1964 film *the gospel according to st. matthew*. a veil accentuates the structure of her face, which is the structure of his face. i've read essays that say this is pasolini likening himself to jesus, but when i saw it, i felt that pasolini used film to visually connect himself to his ideal—women, his mother, *the* mother. in his unfinished posthumously published text, *petrolio*, carlo has to become a woman to attain authenticity. pasolini and his mother shared a household until his death. to break their symbiotic relationship would have rendered her life force inaccessible to him but to sustain it required sacrifice.

when i became pasolini, i could not abide by this conflict.

it won't be surprising to hear that i read a lot, and i began to sense i needed a different kind of book. our local drugstore sold some popular pocket paperbacks. i went in for my regular fare of baseball cards and gum but with a few extra dollars for *psycho-cybernetics* by maxwell maltz, a cosmetic surgeon who developed a system of ideas through which, he claimed, people could remove their emotional scars. he found that even after a successful procedure, many of his patients had unsatisfied expectations. he taught them to visualize the people they wanted to be, and that a person's outer success could never rise above the one visualized internally. i didn't know what a poet was but i began to feel that my imagination could signal the way to a fate different from those in my childhood community. i had not yet encountered the people i wanted to become. pasolini wrote a poem called "prayer to my mother" which i first read in *roman poems*, a selected for english readers published in 1986. i read the book and didn't think it was that good, but then i read it again and thought it was good, but i wanted to write it myself casting myself as pasolini. i called it *pasolini poems*.

in a document posthumously discovered among his papers, pasolini wrote that whenever he was asked to say something about his mother he recalled the same image: walking alone together, arm in arm, outside of the town of sacile, bushes beginning to bud, and blue mountains in the background. he buries his cheek in her fur coat and smells the odor of spring, or what he calls the odor of his life. in his poem, "prayer to my mother," among the great confessional poems, equal to the unpublished entry in candor, he says because you are irreplaceable, the life you gave me is condemned to loneliness

> and i don't want to be alone. i have an infinite
> hunger for love, love of bodies without souls.
>
> for the soul is inside you…

pasolini used poetry to free himself from the authoritarian world of his father and found himself in a different moral system, no less binding. but he didn't pretend to be interested in resolving his inner conflicts—he developed schema for them. one of my mother's habitual expressions was "the world is a dangerous place to live." living in a suburb called "the bubble" with my nuclear family only accentuated this, the bubble served as a microscope. i knew this to be true through living with my father, who had a volatile temper. it was a seamless transition in his mind to yell at me and shortly thereafter approach me jovially, "want to play catch?" but I delivered a daily message to him through my eyes. *my will power is as great as yours.* one of the things he couldn't tolerate was "a half-assed job." i had a lot of anxiety around performing my chores to his satisfaction. when i ran over his newly planted shrubs with the tractor mower and got sent to my room, instead of resolving to do better i resolved to do less and do it slower. i became so inefficient that my mother ended up covering for me.

the first poem in *roman poems* that i wanted to rewrite was "prayer to my mother." pasolini and i are ambassadors from the same land of ruin so the message was similar though in my version i am more accusatory:

> if i were a son i might have the words
> to say how my heart so little resembles
>
> any other love and that you knew
> and made it impenetrable

then i rewrote "rage" directing his defiant tone toward the mother instead of the world.

we had an english springer spaniel for about 6 months, a breed of gun dog traditionally used for flushing and retrieving game. i had been hunting with my father many times and saw that he was a good shot with gun and bow. we got along well in the town of wild rose, where he killed whatever animal was in season, cooked it, and served it. springers are rambunctious and no one in my family properly trained him. my mother wasn't a dog person and was home with him the most. i once witnessed my dad kick him down the stairs. later that week, when the dog misbehaved, i hit his hind end with his leash and was overcome with horror. when my mother, crying, told me that a family from the country was coming to adopt him, i didn't cry. i walked him to an overgrown row of lilac bushes that marked our lot line and said goodbye to him in private.

my parents wanted me to attend a high school called pius, but they didn't insist. my experience at st. alphonsus ungrounded my mother's faith in the church just enough, and my father stopped going through the motions of a believer. he was the first person i heard called a heathen. i conflated this with another notion i had about him. when i was angry with him i would ask my mother if she knew she was married to a cro-magnon man. after a pause, in which she made the decision not to admonish me, we both burst into laughter. there were other incidents where she issued an inside joke in his presence to make him feel out of place. one of her culinary specialties was stuffed artichokes but she wouldn't make one for him saying, "no carciofo for the medigan," "medigan" is italian slang for a person who is not italian like she and his children were. he sat eating his dish of pasta and sauce, his boney brow shielded his eyes so i couldn't detect how he felt.

throughout this story i've wondered why i've omitted the presence of my younger brother. insofar that this is a story about reparation, he is irreproachable, and insofar as our shared parentage, the psychic atmospheres we conjured with and within them were distinct. because he was male, and second-born, he was exempt from the battle that was taking most of their energy, the battle over me. for him the nuclear family became a formal situation rather then a source of emotional sympathy and he learned to look elsewhere for what he needed. however, he ate his stuffed artichoke with his head of thick black hair and his easy-going smile and i suspected that he was getting something that i wasn't, a childhood unfettered by adult concerns. i always thought my mother's habitual expression, "the world is a dangerous place to live," was issued with hope that i would become as fearful as she was. if i were going to be a lesbian, at least i could grow up to be a spinster who would live with her. in fact, i was riddled with fear and suspicion but knew i needed to trick myself into thinking i was someone different, a terrae filius, a son of the earth. the night pasolini was brutalized and murdered, he gave an interview where he said, "we're all in danger." he stopped the interview at dusk and asked that the interviewer leave the questions with him so he could come up with a concluding remark. when i heard "we're all in danger" from pasolini, i was released from my comprehension of a sentiment made to control me and took it to be a statement about world history.

Pasolini Poems :: Divine Mimesis

(2020)

Preface to *Pasolini Poems :: Divine Mimesis*

Szymaszek's Pasolini *Poems :: Divine Mimesis* is a collection of poems based, sometimes loosely (sometimes tightly) on Pier Paolo Pasolini's *Roman Poems*, a conceptual framework she's using for the second time, with a sly nod to his *The Divine Mimesis*.

A fair amount of pointing and prodding is going down. Going down in the poems and going down in the conceptual conceit of responding to beloved forebears. I like being pushed around like this, being narrowed and directed in ways I might not have moved otherwise.

Guided.

Our Virgils here shapeshift. Szymaszek and Pasolini each take turns leading us through the poems, pointing out important references, tripping us on red herrings, breaking small moments like hearts and treasures and generally confounding the unidirectional read of any piece of artwork as a fixed and knowable entity.

Pasolini, in his mimesis, responds to Dante's cantos. Midway through his life he takes a journey through hell riffing on Dante's midlife journey through hell, putting his thing down, flipping and reversing it. There is, in both, a critique of Italian social and political structures and a none-too-disguised consideration of personal structures. What they'd built so far, what plasticity they'd maintained at this midpoint. Szymaszek's midlife journey is through a very different hell.

(And sometimes that hell seems downright gratifying. When Szymaszek writes:

in the desert I just sit and think and in thinking

and using the sky to know time I am mortal

this awareness of mortality doesn't seem harrowing or gothically vulgar but peaceful, bountiful, blessed. And more than gratifying, there are celebratory lines like:

victorious   lesbian   off-grid

that revel in the corporeal, present, radical, personal.)

Szymaszek begins *Pasolini Poems :: Divine Mimesis* with a reference to release, denial and failure. Are these first poems an assault on divinity? A repositioning of divinity as something wholly human? (Holy human.) If what is being recreated is flawed, then must divinity be flawed as well? Or is flawed, perhaps, divine? To be flawed the most holy? And perhaps being an underachiever, as she suggests she is in the poem "Diary," is not a failure but a success. Perhaps to not achieve is the most successful a poet can be as it keeps our scribe in a state of continuous continuing. I've been thinking a lot about 'failure' and I think this series of poems is too (though there's no way to know the ratio of what I bring to the text in relation to what the text brings to me), but the poems and I seem enamored with a sort of ethos—this particular human 'flaw,' the distinctly shameful patina of 'making it big' set against the deep and radical cool of the

pension-less crone.

The devastating, liberating line

middle-aged women don't sell

in "The Desire for Wealth" becomes a Janus word. Janus line? (Perhaps they just will not sell out?)

Failure is just one seam through the hell/not hell of this diving board/homage. Also regularly considered is the concept of money. Money as a humorous/destructive cosmic element. Both the personal implications of need and the public impact of this material on our culture. "The Desire for Wealth II" turns from the personal, in the first "The Desire for Wealth," to the public. The institution's desire for wealth near as searing:

—the inst. makes sure you don't see
other poetries

This poem, with its coy abbreviation, reminds me of Russell Atkins's line "that which gives money takes it away."

Poets (as deity, celebrity, soothsayer, friend, and self) figure prominently in most of Szymaszek's writing and here this reverential handling is perhaps best encapsulated in the lines:

poets with pulsing
hands report
the future is
beyond time

In *Pasolini Poems :: Divine Mimesis*, we are reminded that Szymaszek considers poets a race or class or time of holy people, beings beyond allegiance to vocation.

But aging, community, God, sex and so much walking, are each considered and transformed by Szymaszek's incisive poetics (a poetics that moves from percussive to melodic with speed and precision). Maybe these are the only topics, and if a someone writes about something else, that something else is only a metaphor for, or symbolic of, these pop hits here addressed with such surprising candor and trickery.

And, like *Roman Poems, Pasolini Poems :: Divine Mimesis* ends with death. A possessed death, mapped like an Electric Company animation, cherished, ideated, lightly held in the humor/sorrow that most befits mortality and concern about the curl of one's hair. Is death here climbing Lucifer and wriggling through cracks to emerge from the inferno of our present existence? I guess we won't know for a bit more but I find it a consoling and optimistic ending.

—Stephanie Barber

Diary

I solved the problem of the young queer woman
on the plane by telling her I used to have a very social job
what no one knew including myself
was that when it was over I'd go back to being
an underachiever in a westward town
but this time without anxiety

a famous artist of the lower east side erased his early years
as a poet yet I had thought of him everyday
in a way I only thought about poets
as I passed his old address
a movie theater for years now
splendid day after splendid day

The Holiday Over

I popped my hood to check for pack rats
sundown around 5:30
my mind does the math
Los Angeles   New York   Beirut
imagine my personal space beyond arm's length
to where I send love

sometimes they're called trade rats because they'll leave
one object for one they like better
at supper we felt we were down one fork and the arts
section of the paper   it's low burn chaos
but never us versus them

I discovered I could create light by running
my hand over a blanket   I have heard or imagined
many threats   a group of night cyclists with a boombox
rode by   my ear was hobbled   there isn't going to be
    enough time
in this era   for scar tissue to remodel itself

every night is ancient
and never happens

my banished highness is in the mountains
wearing a janky crown of Christmas lights
and she has tomato feet   a free life

needs to be invented from whole cloth
all this time in a clued-in tomb   time to step out of line
if there is ever to be a night of real sleep

The Lament of the Excavator

to live for past love makes for agony
that is why I live to obliterate time with poetry
as long as there are more things to know
I won't be scammed into thinking I'm inert

walking in the hills as the city lights switch on
we align with our light   and antagonisms are clarified
yesterday I lived for teaching and publishing
today I'm feeling around dark market places

not scared but galled   professors and poets held loveless
by the administration   or becoming the holders of students
I stay in our flat in my overalls   breathing savory desert air
unsure of how much money I will need

and how to earn it   the pace at which I move
a result of those who have moved fast and broke things
trying to subdue anything feral   time   gender
especially any nuanced use of language

I too offend myself when I trip
into the zeitgeist   tribalism   the score of the mall
the world will never be completely before my eyes
but I'm excavating every story I ever dreamed

and am living select passages with a few others who push
themselves to extremes of knowing and loving

Memories of Poverty

because something else still burns in my heart
I keep my life a theater should I live to behold
a post-work society   my midwestern work ethic
has seniority at 35 years   I'll never live that down

> (serving my ethical obligation   defining myself as a
>   social subject
> as we all figured out our relation to each other
> under sickening power…)

I was a nonprofit director   not like I was a surgeon
or a lawyer but here I am drinking buttermilk and eating apples
filling my belly with enzymes   my hackles still raised
a prayer that I be forgotten that leans
on my vitality   yeah I have gone far
a miracle   with my shy and stubborn personality intact

incapable of monetizing my work   judge of nothing   friend
to no judge   and certainly not as a pension-less crone will I ever
bow to lyrical trojan horses of monocracy
clomping out   *follow your bliss*

because something else governs my heart   some muscle
memory of why my grandparents pretended to be not Polish
not Sicilian some dream of an end to conquest
every morning I do something simple like cut an orange
and keep dressing for the studio looking not unlike an artist
and the neighbor woman who is always home

The Wealth of Knowing

but in this country how can we possess
full consciousness when the mongers
maneuver facts out of existence   how do we know
anything?   how do we know what we know

other than through authorizing and validating
our daily experiences of the world   a world
that reveals itself in a language that threatens
the status quo by refusing to tell
so called relatable stories
for capital   MAKE IT AUTHENTIC

write it on your bathtub
carry yourself like a statesperson
as National Archives staff tampers
with photos critical of mongers
BE A MENACE TO REACTION

the past week so many pet cats have passed
and without their eye contact we are the lonelier
the man filling potholes laughs maniacally   even louder
than his truck spitting cement in the alley
behind my writing quarter
where I am not starving like Marlowe
and have not paid with my life like Pasolini

the more desperate the mongers the stronger the fear
of the poet who says

I DO NOT CONSENT TO MANIPULATE
YOUR EMOTIONS

WILL NOT SCARF UP THE ROLE OF HUCKSTER
or
POSE AS A SMOOTH LYRICAL BEING

my tools of discipline are libraries and benches
for human rears under the olive trees   here in late
January desert I know what my ears tell me
the mourning doves are singing again
to what is Franciscan of my soul *in toto*

my capital is almost spent   this situation almost
exhausted   I will always be the owner of what I know

The Privilege of Thinking

when I spent most of my time surviving a city

time passed slowly
and I felt
a little immortal

you can't imagine an end to vigilance
or moving from one miasma to the next

(there was a time "night air" was thought
to cause plague   as a fresh New Yorker
I did catch strep and my mucus was flecked with dirt)

I rode the subway and wrote what I saw
including my own modest wrong-headed theories

in the desert I just sit and think and in thinking
and using the sky to know time I am mortal

The Privilege of Thinking II

beasts dressed as human
smoting free thinkers
I too am going to work
to make a living   a poet!
it's true   praying to
gauzy gods and performing
my own stunts
the bigger the paycheck
the more stink

publishers and journalists
professors and
poets not exempt   hell
even the manager at the cafe
emboldened to let slip
his beastly hand

what is there for me?
            but hey   I think!

                        find a friendly corner
                                sit   and   think

Roman Evening

In the winter months when it's not too hot to be outside
there still aren't many pedestrians   some Thursdays
around midnight a party starts near our house
and we're bothered by bass lines   but never
the trolley bells   at dusk pick-up trucks of men
barrel down the back alley   to what end I don't know
it's citrus harvest time but the neighbors don't collect
them so I help myself to lemons and make more fish
last night a shriek woke me   (though I was already upright
on a wedged pillow   my eyes masked)   I wondered if it
issued from my mouth like when I was a kid   each phase of life
brings something to dream shriek about   each era of rule
but you know they've taken hold of "the fabric" when the young

inhabit the concerns of the old   such as the high school kids
  on a date

who sat by us at the ramen place   (we were also on a date

quietly sharing a beer)   they worried about their taxes

and how as desert kids they were never taught how to swim

should water ever come from rock

Toward the Caracalla Baths

for three nights there was a hard freeze warning

people covered their cactus tips with foam cups
(not the saguaros)

WE had a we covered

we the people

the cold fractures my sense of body

there are better cities but with heat so pervasive

it becomes a home

I'll pretend I'm not here / not part of never been
part of any scene!

a space heater blew into my core
the tub is missing one clawfoot
the wave in my hair mellows like the color

from black to beach foam finally too old to die young

I no longer think about deserving love

held in thought with few who have the ability to address me

I've read about this   the perils of "not making sense"

undeniably trickled down to the niche

the lyric is a fat cat   with a cat whip

keep sights to self

cash sends out an alluring ray of hope   making all kinds of people

poetic   where is my art's ability to critique when used

in such service

(neoliberalism   even the word is hideous)   at the behest

of a nefarious building we impale ourselves on the fence

what do I know of the baths anymore?   sure an age ago with fellow

poets named after saints in the tepidarium

library books in our bags   I had things to gripe about (the church)

and received such empathy

Sex Consolation for Misery

you poets with your secular response to time   that it is homogenous

are ten-hundred devils   trying to replicate the broken world

a virus revealing how broken   will I persuade devils

to come to grips with silence   the metrics of your audience

is a receipt blowing in spring wind   will you exclude yourselves

part crowds with your nudity   walk to the nearest parcel of dirt   land on your face

where new ordinances say honor is dishonor and there are no winners

or luck   for that matter   luck

is outlawed   will your strength ever be lightness

away from school and some relatable drama

will your joy ever be in the tumult of sex

will your sex ever be an origin story with ten-hundred ends

will you ever admit you are a holy wretch

who could be made fully human when so consoled

Triumph of the Night

the oranges in the dirt

by some hand

were collected and put into a box at the curb

the more time I spend with other kinds

of life the more my memory feels segmented

by pith

            and film

I'll take trampled paddles over a lawn

and whatever this category of oblivion is

over being a cool marauder

low square

            mud room

where my trousers are stiffly drying over pipes

and I released a third moth

emboldened by human absence

I imagine javelinas defending the city

coarse salt

            redden and yell

I love Caravaggio but I'll take

Artemisia Gentileschi playing the lute

as the sun sets over Cuk Do'ag / Tucson Mountains

even as we unlearn Darwin I wipe centuries of vengeance

from my chin with a handkerchief

if there is a hell be it the ninth circle

where her defrauders freeze

night low

            body match

the neighbors are tucked away but

fill common air with weed smoke

and I hold my fingers like a sordid little sister

light pumice

        moon slice

The Desire for Wealth

I observe them   people brought up   to a life other than
    mine   fruit

of a different history   my temptation was kinship   when I
    was young

and desperate for kin   but in the similitude of our sexual
    yearnings

was a rat of medieval usury   the final form of US history   in
    the almost

of social relations   you dare speak of me using the language of
    contract

I watched the prayer card with my blood on it burn

and still I spoke   *middle-aged women don't sell*

my toothless howls (poems)   wracking my brain

as to how much life juice poets without a school   protégé   or
    friend

will need to get to next week   a field of shepherds asleep with their utensils and one lamb

I ate my crown and became bilious

barfing on the terracotta that the hallway in this neat old house is haunted

was confirmed by the pizza maker a chat through masks and in my cleanest white

underwear my modesty bygone growing some ego balls

demand respect for choosing to end my knowledge of the women

shrouded in pain and that they never know of my growth

even on morose Sundays I know the names of all of your books

and the history of poetry before you

savor a bite? I've digested the rubies of executive mitigation

my latent and wolfen desire for wealth still

summoned by the smell of a new chair (the kind you sit on)

a chair that rocks you back into history   and creaks "we made it"

with the air and ancient shrewdness of thieves   eminence

can twist you into a way of life that will house

your imagination   violent transformation

il sesso e il cuore   via sex and the heart

(they don't want you to know)   is the only way out

not the tender eternal milking of your sorrow

The Desire for Wealth II

AT THIS UNCERTAIN TIME

(UNCERTAIN – THE LONG-TERM IMPACT TO THE VALUE OF OUR ENDOWMENT)

THE FOUNDATION'S CORE MISSION

IN DIRECT SUPPORT OF POETS

IS TO REMAIN COMMITTED TO OUR PROGRAMS

INTO PERPETUITY

IN RECOGNITION OF THE EXTREME FINANCIAL

CRISIS RESULTING FROM THE UNPRECEDENTED IMPACT

THE UNIVERSITY IS FURLOUGHING EMPLOYEES

WE HAVE SOME OF THE BEST-RUN PRISONS IN THE WORLD

AND I AM CONFIDENT IN OUR ABILITY TO KEEP PRISONERS SAFE

FROM THE PANDEMIC SWEEPING ACROSS THE GLOBE

the poem is a trojan
horse for the institution

the poet is a person
who makes poems for us

morally good and useful
in perpetuity

are you sad that you don't know how to see
other poetries?—the inst. makes sure you don't see
other poetries

I Too Am…

I too am on the way

to a Caracalla bath

of the mind   thinking

with my stupendo privilegio di pensare

(if there is a chance of God

I love myself for the sake of this God)

our exiles lengthened

I look to the fat fertile mountains

suddenly rapt   undisturbed by

the evil of the day   a new billionaire

gets made   the bath I draw

is a blood bath

with the eye of a broken dish

reduce myself to   niente

victorious   lesbian   off-grid

their brand of violence

cannot locate

me in this immaculate shirt

light house slippers

a run-down house high up in full sun

with a few other women not big on chit chat

who broke the arms off the chairs

imagine being anchored to this world

by the thud of lemons

and the voice of a God in a bird on a wire

alone to the bone
alone to the bone

I too am traveling across land

to bask in my belongings

stored beneath a highway

near a waterway

a leak dripping on my cabinet

books   manuscripts   paintings

of anatomically wrong horses

gifted by cruel mannerists

safe in another corner

I sit on a golden cushion

give the cabinet a thousand drawers

maybe I've written enough

but enough with hierarchies

I offered a bit of possible order

a bit of sweetness

A Sentimental Education

who was I?

a grounded child
transformed into
a grounded adult

my presence
a scandal
to myself

to be delivered
into a world
strong-willed
monstrously timid

just say it
the past is
beyond time

an archive
of filmic
surfaces

age rots
joint tissue
titanium
obsessed

divest your inner
meanness they made
citizens ingest
pills the shape
of sugar dollars

love the world
kill thugs dead
loving the world

just say it now
your stockpile
made you mean

like the market
looks forward
like forbearing
poets with pulsing
hands report
the future is
beyond time

acts of everyday
life don't add up
to empyrean domain
a threat (to them) must
hide in the ordinary

if I say it plainly
I don't want to
be dominated

by mean people
so I fashion a childhood
room to die in
with an elegance
formed against
the better-known
hollow class

who charge us with
indecency (clarity of
language) just
say it you don't
exist just because
you survive

The Resistance and Its Light

Thus I came to the days of resistance
with the consciousness of the sun
illuminating the dissolution of my body in middle air

as the government guarantees deadly eve after eve
our household goods in a cart
far from the cities and friends we made

ready to move disguised in the pure light of desert day
I'll tell you I have no cherished memories
but reunite with elephantine drama

I look into the surrounding mountains to see my mother
fretting for my safety as though it were 1985
my sacrilegious fate sealed

having only been harmed by priest   police   or principal
the persecutory edicts I was meant to collude with
to magnetize early death as if a real martyr

bathed in the light of consciousness
while I am slow and rare
justice does not wear a breastplate of patience

the office takes the human
evilly dispositions the human
in the humane division of wealth

sometimes things fall to earth in the form
of light   stars are suns are meteorites
as other forms of light leave

Tears

through brutal force

common sense becomes

underground knowledge

credentialed cynics teach

the outcome is death

with no light

to keep their jobs

one person's resistance shines light

on live tragedy

we are all in danger

the corporation in the desert

casts you into another desert

where water is an image of water

the periphery of the city bleached

a circle of crossbones

the libraries are closed

pot shots at our death our survival

the poets will walk out

of the circle with acrid farewells

and I in the lecture hall seats of today

have a pissy snake in my guts

and a thousand of my tears

evaporate and my blood

is too thick to draw

and my sweat is metallic pins

from the roots of my hair to

the bottom of my feet

a great gushing out

a great weeping of salt

one can claim to not understand

because it is common knowledge

which is forbidden

pierced by another hundred tears

another martyrdom that would prove useless

if I made a grab for that epic light

my immediate fate releases me

from any attempt to explain myself

I am an adolescent and this

is an unknown Rome

for KA

To the Red Flag

you were waved in a fight

for the eight-hour work day

when that seemed humane

strung behind Medieval ships

to signal—will fight to death

your red has been the blood of calves

red flag

they're packing our wounds with money

old wounds will bleed pennies

no—they are wounding us and stowing money

replicating wound banks

my shoulders a hedge of evergreens

between their party and my pantry

in a pinch you are the aftermath of a dry nose

and the poorest can wave you

Fragment: To Death / To Pasolini

I was born to an eventful summer

a man with money got away with manslaughter

of a woman and not many years later

money murdered you and got away

in one of its many sports cars

I've tried to understand you circling me

sometimes an aura other times an astral

speck sometimes my peers leave

with you and family doesn't want to talk

the person is gone with their story

and we coagulate in the wake of their light

independently and I come no closer

I return to your poetry an isolated

bad-mouthed woman

free of most norms

including denial of you

you are not close to me now but within

I make you deal with the crone crown

in an angry state   A LIVID POETRY

crown my liver

every real act of the world is a great poem

am I healthy? — my body does as it wishes

believe in its sovereignty soundtrack

teenagers in black who laugh

at adults who collude with rich murderers

Rage

I go to the sliding door

and see a Marian shrine beneath

a tree   a white dog that looks like a wolf

and a vegetable garden   an old turntable

plays hymns that were forbidden   *let us join a cohort*

on harpsicord   an acre of rural tranquility

but we need not strain to feel the foreigner's search

for work and bread   and just beyond we see

fascist building sites with yellow tumbling wigs

a sepulchral garage   armored cars   powered by

wind

Mary   the wolf   the garden   are phantasms

ruins

her death was peaceful took the age off her

already inexplicably young-looking century-old face

light   gold   light   nurse   nothing

came over me listening to a poet read about Nancy

Reagan's hair   a locus of pestilence

FINGERS CROSSED

some flock of birds heard her mouth

her nickname translated "noise"

wish for holy violence

to make a graceful act of revenge / and punish a thousand wrongs in a single day

I pause the video on her dead mouth

sitting on a step surrounded by dirt and scrub

hushed fraternities   airborne virus   my mouth covered

she never even looked out the window with a nice view

and an American flag

old knot

wet rose

of my existence

where her remains breathe

arm
pit in-
stant

you think you smell your mother

it's the demon of rage

detaching and whirling on its own

grooming us masters of our time

in a public billionaire bone dump to-be

her roses are pink

I am a poet in my twenties   both a little deaf

internal turbine   the victory of exploding private lives

vomit in their faces

I can't pretend now that I don't know the world

or the way it wants me to be

plastic pumpkin signals

Eastern season

        did she know arid inferno

        dry furor

I am over 50 and new as a youth

who only knows that she is new

and in agreement with her rage

for NB (1920–2020)

I Work All Day

I work all day like a hip priest

and at night I wander the house on the slats

that don't creak reading the tea leaves

at the back of my skull

frequency of rose bouquets

hung stalk-first to dry

mark every sill as if to say

someone with a heart still lives here

the sound of street racing mobs come down on my calm
    courage

they want us to be like scientists this the rational

outcome of their experiment but I when I watch myself

with camera-eye

being massacred

my ancestral blood flies

a flock of crows upon the etched faces

of the treacherous

it is not my job to study their political violence

of which we are always before

but to write all day

with painstaking attention to each line

and how I love

the people I love

and how I hate

the revving newborn fascist

how I celebrate by releasing unforgiving word bundles

that rise into the civic sky

Prayer to My Mother

it's hard to find the voice of the child
at this stage in life and what has been at the heart

of my sorrow feels like a dog-eared book
I'll never read again

is it so terrible to say aloud
I had the will to replace you

but even that condemned me to a kind of solitude
that preserved an underlying commitment to you

an infinite hunger for more than companionship
with bodies housing lost souls

as the only way to feel alive the only form I knew
but now that is over as new mothers are made

and you and I survive in the confusion
a life reborn outside of mothering outside of reason

I cannot beg you or anyone not to desire death during this
horrific time
as your mother took her leave in a hearse with an Italian flag

that would not have been among her wishes
her rigored hand cocked in dissent covered with lace

I can see that we're all here together now
and in every future September…

The Search for a Home

I'm searching for the house where I'll be buried
the real estate in towns outside cities up 100%
the only thing gathering is paperwork

in this game of musical chairs I was one of the standing
poet with a round face baked by the sun and salt hair
no one in charge is taking their organization in my direction

god it's an upsetting day when life is forbidden
when mountains are on fire again and polling places allow guns
the city feels like an enemy city

so I look for a house that I no longer want
to beat the rugs of my anguish
let this be my last youthful reaction a menopause of reaction

troubling with an artichoke for dinner to eat the middle velvet
let's see what is here today that wasn't here yesterday
my sorrow outweighs my acceptance

and today more than yesterday my fear exalts me
in strange October heat I float to the market (masked) for meat
where it once bustled with some sense of civic joy

another palimpsest of a city of the past thrown on top
when the working class supported their people with one job
making steel or delivering milk like my granddads

every place I've lived I've watched mirrored towers appear
I'd really like to see the planners of these dumps
for the de-animated who see themselves reflected back

no eyes no ears no mouths
homes for people with
no nerves

balconies designed for non-use the technical and ethical
dysfunction always equivalent the autocrat has one eye
in his pocket and it winks and thinks it can bless people

so where then to find my studio
which plants itself with an energy all its own
where then to find my home

"dreamt-of nest of my poems" which I need like I need Pasolini
Gramsci's Ashes
and *Poem In the Shape of a Rose*

one who people like to say predicted his murder as if a seer
and not a queer whose nonconformity was "bothersome to
practically everybody"
thus he made a home with his mother and cousin outside of
Rome

I fill out the forms of the world and leave
too many blanks people are bored by those who endure
maybe when you need to know how it's done

you won't be able to find anyone in a fixed residence
ancient world to future world conversing in an elided fashion
I could play up the part of angry woman just to live

in this region where the concept of summer has collapsed in
    the pyre
with other fictions that confirm our being
so the house I'm looking for will be – why not – a basement

or a shed where I can continue to draw with charcoal
and dirty my apron with dust I already have a twitch
a technical intuition to layer myself in the danger calls of birds

maybe I'll muster some gratitude for the deformed hearts of
    conformists
deformed not by their capital but through loving exclusion
the earth is the center of their universe

we are forced from one position into the next then another
and through grace one creates a new style
to feel so different and lost

But It Was a Naked and Swarming Italy

I worked voraciously in New York City with a completely

naturalized suffering and thus my poetry-dreams

were kept intact   it was even fun to write about

if you can recall my raucous laughter   and I entertained

the idea that the city might depend

on poets documenting its streets while walking to and from work

our reality demon blessedly devouring literary nostalgia

now I know I have a calling with no church

yet in agreement with Pasolini in his naked and swarming Italy

of jasmine and poor soup   in poetry is a solution to everything

our role then   to lace into lifetimes of tyranny

solving in our day to day

finding your glasses on your head

palming the pendants of our brilliant dead

in my dusty exodus I who cut a stable and sane figure

sweat the sweat of a traitor

to language hatched by prolific politicos

are you willing to let your body go?

wring out your rags

in the shadows of what they have named action

Civil Song

try to remember our cheeks as they were
after being kissed for the first time
someone who excited us outside
a bookstore   a little older
their frayed collar and falter
hinting at a world of discredited citizens

summon to mind our last few years
without price and before any
of our time was extracted from us
when we wrote in our diaries
then our diaries became poetry
that announced our spirited day to day
hurling shoes into the gut of their perverse logic

see young citizens coming together election week

learning how to care for bullet wounds

the week virus cases break the global daily record

never lulled into a false state of trust

they are naturally ready

to correspond with us

The Presence

to Maria Callas

every morning the tragedy of existence begins
again the shutters rattling from a divine wind
that blows for only a few witnesses

who know what matters is a story
that has to go on claw-like in manner
you tore your voice to ribbons

pursuing something more important to artistry
than beautiful sound
(eccentric imagination and real passion)

your
heavy body   voice
heavenly body

set the goddamn rules
till the capricious wind changed direction
dissipated and you managed to mother

yourself through loss in a near-silent film
set in a prehistoric intelligence where
all rituals were real experiences

we may call ourselves   demigods
queens
or centaurs

opening and closing the shutters with our hands
(or four feet) conducting the airborne sickness

Friulian Paintings

coatless in the creosote air
I was aimless on my evening walk
my breath humid in my mask walking

till I had a sense that I no longer existed
or I still existed in other cities too

  imagination in air
    held in clouds
      the smell of imagination hitting asphalt
        opening passages

I was on my evening walk kicking up dust
the sounds of people celebrating
in the streets of New York City

  ringing my ears
    a happy horn blew in the distance
      the sky phosphoreal

neighbor talked on speaker phone outside
airing her legal troubles and smoking
casita after casita
if we lived in this casita…

maneuvered around a beat-up paddle cactus on the path
    lavender patches and black
        undid every defense of the heart

I did notice her things on the ledge
moved after her last political wish was half-realized
the leaves of elders rustled all around

*

I read Friulian willows as widows whose wood does not drop
in storms think of Kollwitz who knew to use wood
and ink to depict held anguish

the mountains in every direction are stark
provide no narratives and countless perspectives
I turned west and remembered our pagan evening

that yielding of ours a festive measure of childish heart
that made the city seem like an everyday piazza
our love was so hot and wise it galvanized us into hags

with three nights of perfect knowledge of each other
    followed by ages of getting to know each other

        mental drives through eastern corridors of
            blood red webbed sugar maples

I still try to look my best in soft pants
dress for a work day at my desk readying me for a walk
the news still shocks me I am still falling from grace

smells of people's suppers penetrated my mask
tugged forward by puffs of newly legal weed
shrouded porch-side plosive clusters

  canned salmon
    coffee with plum notes
      rice and cocoa

*

the wind felt other-planetary displacing dirty earth air
dotting it with energy to upend the mortal stasis
each side licks their fingers and holds to the sky

there is no damp light of the sea east of me
nor deep blue of the lake but this mountain that looks
as if you could unravel yourself forever and not reach it

  redefine festive
    an unreal something
      an eternal street fair

        a civic song
          thrumming in basilic veins

visitation by the ghost of hot adolescent sex
in colors renounced for brown
bent over like an expressionist
willing to take your meaning
I headed south toward the colony of stray
cats in mesquite trees and on top of broken air conditioners
the largest gathering I've seen in months

the wind carried the glaucous stench of herb
torched my passages an everlasting orange sun
orange with California fire

    black and purple drape drawn
        a sweet clot to seize
            the over handled dough dream

spotted a few people reading on their porches
feeling Pauline missing the Corinthians
upon seeing Fortunatus and friends
happy *because these men have made up for your absences*

*

and the wind blew an aluminum chair down
the main drag night skidded in real time
what a taste of death

moments nullified of clairvoyance
presence is worth years of clarity
a confused time starts to clear up in memory

imagine a mother-in-law spoiling your life
or rather a spouse's devotion to her
spousal abandon leading to religious ecstasy

    she could only die after a cruciform melody
        but leaving me to love who I love with street slang
            baccala and brandy latch

*

and then while walking and remembering all of the cities
I realized a city can be repellent
it repels me as in won't have me

beyond surface smile and wave
people warned New York will chew you up and
spit you out but New York loved me

I still exist there because some New
Yorkers still love me there
living more fully here in exquisite

    paradox
        in the provinces
            far from money

not driven to speak money
language to get golden bones
not drivable into an institution

    too
        vivid
            idiom

I became lost in dawn and adobe vespers
imagine saying the same prayer for 75 years
history gave her hell

a violent urge toward expression inflated her hands
shaken by fear of her sins
every object around her seemingly inflated

household objects formed a parade of floats
a smiling seam ripper a winking rolling pin
a place and a people rumored festive
covered in the dust of chaff in the sun

infamous west wind blew me further
from every home winnowed me
from those who would be kin
if they could permit me safe growth

The Song of the Bells

when the days were so outwardly repetitious
there was the public measure of Lutheran bells
sounding noon behind the house
a young man repeated "hello?" at the open door
wanted to use the phone
and in that instant I didn't know if a day
has passed or another year
bejeweled he told me not to be afraid of him
                I told him not to be afraid of me

The Day of My Death

in a city
if there be a city
in a town
if there be a town
by the sea
if the sea has not engulfed the city
or in the desert
on the outskirts of fire
I'll drop dead
under the sun
my face a blonde whorl
and I'll close my eyes
signaling to gothic birds
I am their splendor

under a warm coat of snow
under a cold green pile of felled saguaro
under the spell of clawing lobsters
I'll fall into my death's mouth
heaving inward my language
leaving untraceable god lines
for beautiful gender-
queers who will run in the refracted
light I have just lost
flying from schools if there be schools
still caring that their curls be disarranged
upon their brows

Notes on the Poems

Pasolini said "we are all in danger" in his last interview a few hours before he was murdered. It was published in *La Stampa* on November 8, 1975.

Italicized words in "Toward the Caracalla Baths" (2020) are by Robert Lax from *A Hermit's Guide to Home Economics.*

Italicized words in "Rage" (2020) are from Petrarch's *The Canzoniere* #2.

"The Presence" incorporates language from Vincent Canby's review of *Medea* in *The New York Times*, October 29, 1971.

Acknowledgments

Pasolini Poems was published in 2005 by Cy Press with a second edition of 200 printed in 2006. I'm forever thankful to editor Dana Ward for finding me, when people were harder to find, after reading a few of the poems in the journal *Aufgabe*. Other Pasolini Poems also appeared in *Boog City*, *Crayon*, and *Rust Buckle*. A letterpress chap featuring 5 of the poems was printed in an edition of 35 by David Pavelich's Answer Tag Home Press (2004). Broadsides were printed by Brenda Iijima's Portable Press at Yo-Yo Labs and John Tyson's Singlepress.

11 Poems from Divine Mimesis :: Pasolini Poems was published by Blazing Stadium in 2020 in an edition of 40. Some of the *Divine Mimesis* poems have appeared in the journals *Blazing Stadium*, *Can We Have Our Ball Back*, *Castle Grayskull*, *Elderly*, *The Poetry Project's House Party*, *Nomaterialism*, *Poems by Sunday*, and *Prolit*. Pieces from "A Sentimental Education," in different versions, were published in *Vanitas*.

So many people have offered meaningful encouragement when I started writing these poems in 2004, at a time when I had published very little. Etel Adnan, who also loved Pasolini, and is someone whose work I understand in the civic poet tradition, became a mentor and friend. This book is for her.

The prose sections of this book were arduous to write. When I thought it might be quits for PPP and me, the following people's care, or just interest, helped me stay with the writing: Renee Gladman, Barbara Hammer, Vincent Katz, Gail

Scott, and Bill Kushner, among others. In 2012, I was invited to perform with Pasolini scholar Ara H. Merjian for a multimedia event entitled "Pasolini's Body: Poetics, Politics and Performance" which further sparked my will to stay with the project.

I've been fortunate to have Matt Longabucco, Allison Grimaldi Donahue, and Brandon Brown as recent close readers. Deep thanks to the filmmakers, writers, and former Milwaukeeans Stephanie Barber for writing the preface to *Pasolini Poems :: Divine Mimesis*, and Jennifer Montgomery for the preface to the 2005 chapbook.

Divine Mimesis was written under quarantine in Tucson, AZ, with my partner, the poet Kimberly Alidio, the closest of readers. One big difference between the poems written in 2004 and those in 2020 is the presence of love in the house.

Finally, thank you to Lawrence Giffin and Christopher Catanese for their strong editorial vision both for Golias Books and *The Pasolini Book*.

The Pasolini Book is Stacy Szymaszek's sixth book of poetry. Her book *Famous Hermits* will be also be published in 2022. She is the recipient of a 2014 New York Foundation for the Arts Fellowship in Poetry and a 2019 Foundation for Contemporary Arts grant in poetry. From 2007–2018, she was the director of The Poetry Project at St. Mark's Church in New York City. She currently lives in the Hudson Valley where she is an educator and a freelance consultant for arts and social justice nonprofits.

Golias Books seeks to promote and circulate poetry that avails itself of a diverse array of registers, modes, genres, and formal possibilities—poetry that traffics in the remoter realms of what has traditionally been called poetics. We are interested in longer poems that develop more extended narrative or discursive arcs than that of the dilatory epiphany, in poetry as argument or architecture or assemblage, in poetry that means and does rather than poetry that expresses. At the same time, while the lessons of the previous few generations' emphasis on experimentation are well taken, we seek to explore an intuition that something of value may have been lost along with earlier humanisms' concern with ethical, political, and aesthetic judgment; therefore, while abjuring reactionary or conservative atavisms, we are interested in revitalizing historical poetic forms that may help us expand the narrow demesne within which contemporary poetry largely confines itself.